Robert Cormier

Other titles in the *Authors Teens Love* series:

Ray Bradbury
Master of Science Fiction and Fantasy
ISBN-13: 978-0-7660-2240-9
ISBN-10: 0-7660-2240-4

Gary Paulsen
Voice of Adventure and Survival
ISBN-13: 978-0-7660-2721-3
ISBN-10: 0-7660-2721-X

Orson Scott Card
Architect of Alternate Worlds
ISBN-13: 978-0-7660-2354-3
ISBN-10: 0-7660-2354-0

Philip Pullman
Master of Fantasy
ISBN-13: 978-0-7660-2447-2
ISBN-10: 0-7660-2447-4

Roald Dahl
Author of Charlie and the Chocolate Factory
ISBN-13: 978-0-7660-2353-6
ISBN-10: 0-7660-2353-2

Jerry Spinelli
Master Teller of Teen Tales
ISBN-13: 978-0-7660-2718-3
ISBN-10: 0-7660-2718-X

Paula Danziger
Voice of Teen Troubles
ISBN-13: 978-0-7660-2444-1
ISBN-10: 0-7660-2444-X

R. L. Stine
Creator of Creepy and Spooky Stories
ISBN-13: 978-0-7660-2445-8
ISBN-10: 0-7660-2445-8

C. S. Lewis
Chronicler of Narnia
ISBN-13: 978-0-7660-2446-5
ISBN-10: 0-7660-2446-6

J. R. R. Tolkien
Master of Imaginary Worlds
ISBN-13: 978-0-7660-2246-1
ISBN-10: 0-7660-2246-3

Joan Lowery Nixon
Masterful Mystery Writer
ISBN-13: 978-0-7660-2194-5
ISBN-10: 0-7660-2194-7

E. B. White
Spinner of Webs and Tales
ISBN-13: 978-0-7660-2350-5
ISBN-10: 0-7660-2350-8

Robert Cormier

Author of *The Chocolate War*

Ann Angel

Enslow Publishers, Inc.
40 Industrial Road
Box 398
Berkeley Heights, NJ 07922
USA

http://www.enslow.com

Acknowledgments
With special gratitude to Robert Cormier's wife Connie,
and to his daughters Bobbi, Chris, and Renee, who gave
generously of their time and stories to make this biography possible.

Library of Congress Cataloging-in-Publication Data

Angel, Ann, 1952–
    Robert Cormier : author of The chocolate war / [Ann Angel].
        p. cm. — (Authors teens love series)
    Includes bibliographical references and index.
    ISBN-13: 978-0-7660-2719-0
    ISBN-10: 0-7660-2719-8
    1. Cormier, Robert. 2. Authors, American—20th century—Biography—
Juvenile literature. 3. Young adult fiction—Authorship. I. Title.
PS3553.O653Z68 2006
813'.54—dc22
[B]

                                        2006022848

Printed in the United States of America

10 9 8 7 6 5 4 3 2 1

To Our Readers: We have done our best to make sure all Internet addresses in
this book were active and appropriate when we went to press. However, the
author and publisher have no control over and assume no liability for the material available on those Internet sites or on other Web sites they may link to. Any
comments or suggestions can be sent by e-mail to comments@enslow.com or to
the address on the back cover.

Illustration Credits: All interior images courtesy of the Cormier family.

Cover Illustration: Courtesy of the Cormier family (foreground); June Ponte
(background).

Contents

Chapter 1

Dare to Disturb the Universe

The first young adult novels fed readers the ideals of romance and hope. They were peopled with characters whose lives reflected rosy and false worlds for readers. But one writer, Robert Cormier, wrote his first young adult novel to reflect a world where problems are not so neatly resolved. He wrote about difficult choices in teen lives and allowed his endings to come out of his characters' inability to right a world turned upside down by violence and grief.

In fact, realistic young adult novels might only exist because Robert Cormier's *The Chocolate War* dared to disturb the universe of children's book publishing. But Cormier, known by friends and colleagues as Bob, once admitted, "The novel was almost stillborn and existed for more than a year in a kind of literary no-man's-land."[1] Seven major publishers rejected it in 1972 and 1973. Some felt the novel was too complicated, others felt it had too many characters, still others said the ending lacked hope. Many editors believed teenagers of the 1970s would find the downbeat ending too difficult to accept; the plot was too violent. At least one editor said the manuscript was not quite an adult novel, but too sophisticated to be a juvenile novel. Other editors claimed the story was too unbelievable. And most frustrating for Cormier, some editors simply rejected it with, "Not for us."

One editor expressed interest, but only if some changes were made, particularly to the ending. Cormier decided not to change or revise the novel because he wanted to realistically portray the escalating tension and violence caused by teenager Jerry Renault's stubborn refusal to sell candy for his prep school's annual sale. Cormier said this was not a heroic gesture but an act of innocence. "I knew nothing of the young adult market, was unaware of its then traditions and taboos, the domination of 'safe' stories with role-model heroes walking off into the sunset of happy endings," he said.[2]

The amazing thing was that, while Cormier never doubted that his novels would find an audience, he did not set out to write specifically for teens.[3] Once he found this audience, he was loyal to them and made sure that he gave them the sort of honest and realistic fiction they came to expect from him.[4]

Cormier explained, "I do not regard myself as a 'young adult' author. I think any story or novel, if written honestly and without regard for a specific audience, will set off shocks of recognition across a broad range of readers," he said. "I discovered the 'young adult' audience only after I had written *The Chocolate War*. But the discovery of this audience has been a delight. There is no audience so responsive, so caring, so quick to be passionate about a book, so innocently critical and so marvelously appreciative."[5]

The novel was inspired by Cormier's son Peter, who, after discussing it with his parents, decided not to participate in his school's annual chocolate sale as a matter of principle. Although there were no repercussions for Peter, Cormier recalled how his mind played "what if" the day Peter returned to school to refuse to participate. What if school bullies attempted to force someone to sell the chocolate? What if the power of a bully was dependent upon it? What if no one stood to take a character's defense in a situation like this?[6]

In Cormier's mind, fiction came from taking characters down paths that twist and turn. One decision leads his characters to more choices that can change the direction of the character's life for good or bad.[7] At first, in *The Chocolate War,* Jerry, chooses not to sell chocolates and is encouraged in this by members of his school's secret society, the Vigils. He continues to refuse after they order him to sell and even though they taunt and persecute him.[8] Cormier's role as the writer of this novel was to follow Jerry's choices, to push the possibilities in realistic and sometimes frightening ways, to their inevitable conclusions.[9]

Exaggerated instances of harassment at the hands of peers from Cormier's own life fed into the horror of the Vigils' torment of Jerry. In one scene Jerry is ordered to help destroy a classroom. Cormier came up with this idea while at one of his children's schools. He noticed a coat hook that barely hung to the wall by a loosened screw. What if, he wondered, someone purposely loosened the hook? What if someone were to unscrew all the furnishings? This scene entered into *The Chocolate War* when the Vigils charge their victims to loosen the screws in every chair and desk, and even the chalkboard. When students come into the classroom the next morning and touch them the whole room collapses.[10]

Although Jerry goes along with the prank, his continued refusal to partake in the chocolate sale turns into a school-wide war that even draws in power-hungry administrators who pressure the Vigils to end Jerry's challenge. In raising the stakes, Cormier creates a novel that ends only when the war escalates to a bitter end for Jerry.[11]

The Chocolate War was not Cormier's first novel. While working as a columnist and editor for his local newspaper, Cormier had written three previous adult novels. This was the first for young adults.

Now and at the Hour, a semi-autobiographical novel that retraced his father's death from cancer, came out in 1960.[12] "We were very close," Cormier recalled. "He was going through a puzzling time and I felt his world narrowing. I was angry about it."[13]

His second adult novel, *A Little Raw on Monday Mornings*, a tale of a lonely widow who becomes pregnant, was published in 1963.[14] *Take Me Where the Good Times Are*, a novel that mulls over what would happen if a man in a poor house received an inheritance, was published in 1965.[15]

Each of these novels shared the one trait that made Cormier's young adult novels stand out: flawed heroes who cannot always make the best choices.[16]

The author once described why his writing shifted from adult characters to a focus on young adults: "I did not consciously set out to write about young people. But there came a time when my home was occupied by a son and two daughters in the throes of adolescence [Cormier's fourth child followed ten years behind the other three]. Their lives seesawed between ecstasy and despair, often during one single afternoon. They fell in and out of love as swiftly and flamboyantly as the seasons change. They lived on the knife-edge of emotional crisis. And all of this mattered to them. They could telescope a lifetime in an afternoon at the beach. And I realized they were living a life far more exciting, more excruciating, more intriguing than mine. And I came to write more and more about them, matching their comings and goings with memories of my own. But I did not set out to write for them but about them. In fact, I felt like a robber, stealing their emotions and translating them into fiction for my own purposes, for other people to read. I hoped they would forgive me if I did it with compassion and a measure of tenderness."[17]

Just as his earlier novels were written around the hours he worked his fulltime job, *The Chocolate War* was written weekday evenings and Saturday mornings at Cormier's Leominster home. From 1966 through 1971 Cormier also worked at *The Fitchburg Sentinel and Enterprise*. His children fell asleep to the sounds of their father at the typewriter. "My memories of Dad during my teen years are still so vivid," said Chris Cormier Hayes, who was in high school when her father wrote *The Chocolate War*. After coming home from nights out with friends, a party, a movie, or dances, Cormier's children would track the sound of the typewriter keys clicking on paper into his door-less office for late night chats. "What strikes me most is how many of my friends loved talking to him. . . . That was what was so great about our father. He really had the ability to understand and accept what was going on in our (and our friends!) emotional lives."[18]

It was during these late nights that the dark days of Jerry Renault's war took shape. At one point in the novel, published in 1974, Jerry contemplates a poster hanging in his locker, reading,

"Dare to Disturb the Universe." In refusing to sell the candy, Jerry dares to disturb his own universe when he challenges the school's secret society, the Vigils.[19]

This was not a difficult novel to write, Cormier said. Rather, it was a novel that simply unfolded in the way the characters behaved. There was no happy ending, not even a moment of hope, because, as Cormier saw it, that is not always the way of the world.[20] Still, Cormier demonstrated compassion and empathy for his characters. As he said, "Writing the novel was a labor of love."[21] Cormier did not necessarily believe that evil might "conceivably carry the day," rather *The Chocolate War* is a novel "which views human beings as victims of social and natural forces."[22]

Despite the gritty realism and unflinching consequences portrayed in his novels, Cormier was a kind gentleman, according to all who knew and loved this newspaperman who lived his entire life in Leominster, Massachusetts. Connie Cormier recalls that her husband's relationship to his family, friends, and community had a tremendous impact on his writing. "He was a man of extreme compassion and tolerance. He accepted all viewpoints, listened to everyone's opinions, and was astute enough to know we all suffer through the feelings of insecurity and self-doubt. He remembered the emotions of adolescence, both the exhilarations and the anguishes and could, on some level, identify himself with his characters."[23]

While most cheered Cormier's first young adult

novel, reactions were not all pleasant. Many others believed the book portrayed too many "repellent" aspects of the American culture. To some minds, the book contained an abundance of violence and sexual activity. It portrayed many adults as evil. The book was officially challenged in 1976 when Connie Manter, a teacher in Groton, Massachusetts, assigned the book to her ninth grade class. Some parents complained, taking the matter up with the school board and attempting to remove the book from the classroom. In Irmo, South Carolina, one high school principal attempted to remove the book from the tenth grade reading list. While in the Midwest, a group called Parents for Basic Education formed a committee of Lapeer, Michigan parents to remove this book from reading lists while also working to gain control of books on future lists.

Even though *The Chocolate War* sold beyond anyone's wildest expectations, it would continue to be challenged into the 80s and 90s and even now.[24]

Cormier spoke out against organized efforts to censor or challenge his work and other authors' work. He did not want his neighbors telling him what he or his children could or could not read. He felt strongly that, while censorship might increase sales, young people would read his books for all the wrong reasons.[25]

He explained why he wrote novels about "terrible things" and why young adults are drawn to them: "It's possible to be a peaceful man, to abhor violence, to love children and flowers and old Beatles songs and still be aware of the confusions and abrasions this world inflicts on us. Not to write happy endings does not mean the writer does not believe in them. Literature should penetrate all the chambers of the human heart, even the dark ones."[26]

Cormier's youngest child, Renee Cormier Wheeler, now a mother of teens herself, recalls her father as a man who was sympathetic to the struggles of childhood and adolescence. "He had the knack for making ordinary things feel like an adventure, such as exploring a dead end street or finding a new shortcut." Renee also recalls that, although he became known as a writer who portrayed tragic heroes and anti-heroes in their darkest hours and moments, he had a wonderful sense of humor. "He loved old jokes and bad puns. Dinnertime conversations often revolved around word games and jokes. He loved rhyming riddles, which we called 'nitty gritties,' and he could tell a joke better than anyone I've ever met."[27]

The Chocolate War's publication in 1974 was significant because it marked "the debut of a singular talent on the stage of young adult literature" and it set free the subject of despair. Michael Cart, a writer who studies the trends and development of young adult writing, described Cormier's influence: "Cormier had the courage to write a novel of thematic weight and substance that actually suggested that there might be no happy endings in young adult lives; that conventional morality

A Great Humor

Renee Cormier Wheeler recalls that when she was growing up, ten years younger than her next oldest sibling, her father was already a fulltime writer. After school and vacations, she spent a lot of her time visiting libraries and bookstores with her dad. But her favorite memories are still of his sense of humor and the way it would take over at family meals. His jokes proved to get the best of everyone, even him. "One night at dinner he laughed so hard he flipped his chair over backwards! He lay there on the floor, feet dangling in the air, somehow, miraculously, unhurt, and still laughing. My siblings and I all agree that dad gave us the gift of a sense of humor, something we've been thankful for our whole lives."[28]

might not prevail; that evil might be real and even institutionalized; and that there are powerful, faceless forces that will destroy us if we disturb them. This may not be a revolutionary concept in the history of deterministic philosophy, but in the 1970s, it *was* revolutionary as a view of the world upon which to construct a young adult novel. And it opened enormous areas of thematic possibility for writers who would come after Cormier."[29]

While some reviewers were not quite sure how to deal with the dark ending of *The Chocolate War*, the novel was generally applauded for the realistic and daring perspective it took. *Kirkus Reviews*, which gave the novel a starred review, said, "Mature young readers will respect the uncompromising ending that dares disturb the upbeat universe of juvenile books."[30]

The *School Library Journal*, which also gave the novel a starred review said, "The characterizations of all the boys are superb, and Cormier is especially sharp in showing the boys' relationship to and manipulation of each other . . . unique in its uncompromising portrait of human cruelty and conformity."[31]

The novel received many awards including a Best Novel for Young Adults by the American Library Association.[32]

According to Connie Cormier, her husband acknowledged that, while he seemed to grow up knowing he was a writer, the publication of *The Chocolate War* was a turning point in his career. "He was a voracious reader, and I think his newspaper background stayed with him. He was always looking for stories, a different angle."[33]

Over thirty years after its publication, *The Chocolate War* continues to be a popular literary choice among high school students and is often assigned in English literature classes. But controversy surrounding the novel still exists. In fact, Cormier's subsequent novels would add to the firestorm of discussions over what is and is not acceptable literature for teens.

Young people, Cormier said, remained constant reminders in his writing of his own vulnerable years.

Keep on Writing

Connie Cormier recalls that even after Bob's great success, he always treated writing like a job. "He had a routine and every morning found him at his typewriter whether he had anything to write or not. He kept a folder with ideas. Writing was not only his job, but a way in which he understood life and expressed himself in relation to the rest of the world.

"When his words were singing and the writing was going smoothly, he was joyful. When the words would not come he'd just stick with it. He'd walk the floor, take a ride to a library, meet friends at a walking field. He used to advise young people who wrote him that they just 'keep on writing' even when what they had to say did not seem very interesting. Getting the words and emotions down on paper was what was important. The 'spark' would eventually happen."[34]

He said, "And I realize that I am still vulnerable. The borders between childhood and young adulthood, between youth and age, are too blurred, too undefined. I've never been able to trace my own border crossings. I am 18 forever and also 32 and 14 and 52 and 21—and I would not want it to be any other way."[35]

Chapter 2

Life at the Comb Factory

It seems a little ironic that the writer who would grow into a master of books about tragic heroes, difficult choices, and violence lived such an ideal life. But Bob Cormier was born of parents who provided their children with three generations of family and love.

Cormier's grandparents, both French Canadians, met in Quebec. Edmund Cormier, born on March 25, 1864 in St. Felix de Kinsey and Eleanore Charland, born on September 28, 1869 in St. Cloud, were married in on October 27, 1890 in Richmond, Quebec.

The young couple was keenly aware of the ways in which the Industrial Revolution was changing the world. They decided to leave their French Canadian farm community to find work in

the United States factories that had begun to
spring up along the country's rivers. The couple
headed to Worcester County in Massachusetts
where the winding Nashua River provided the per-
fect location for manufacturing.

Cotton and paper mills, a straw bonnet factory,
a shirt factory, a few leather boot and shoe compa-
nies, and at least one comb factory, dotted the
river's shores. Irish, Italian, and French Canadian
immigrants were creating communities among the
region's hills.[1]

Eleanore and Edmund settled into their own
tenement in the French Hill district of Leominster
where Edmund purchased a horse and wagon to
collect rubbish from stores and businesses.

Here, the couple raised ten children, and,
as their children grew and married, each couple
moved into tenements, called triple-deckers,
owned by their parents.[2]

One son, Lucien Joseph Cormier, born on
August 28, 1898, worked in the local comb factory.
He met Irma Collins while dating Irma's older sister. Lucien and Irma (born of French and Irish
parents on November 7, 1900), began keeping
company when she was only 15 years old. They
married five years later in 1920. Then Lucien
moved Irma into one of his close-knit family's
tenements.

Almost three years after they were married,
Irma gave birth to a son, Norman. Robert
Edmund, born January 17, 1925, followed short-
ly after. Cormier, born in Fitchburg, grew up in the

French Hill district of Leominster. His little brother, Leo, who only lived three years, was born in 1926.

Leo's death, when Bob was almost five, was one that saddened Bob. As the older brother, he had taken good care of this golden-haired little brother when they played outdoors.[3] Bob always had vivid memories of the room his brother died in; of the way he was sent to fetch his grandfather that sorrowful morning in fall of 1929; even how he chose to cut through backyards to get his grandfather as quickly as possible.[4] The settings for many of Bob's novels would later reflect these scenes from his own childhood in fictional towns called Monument and Frenchtown.

Despite his brother's death, the family continued to grow. A sister Gloria was born in 1929. John was born in 1931. Ann was born in 1933, and twins Connie and Charles followed in 1939.

Bob's father worked in the Leominster comb factory. While harsh working conditions were experienced by Bob's father and uncles, his own life was pretty serene. Living in triple-deckers owned by his grandfather, Bob was able to run upstairs to visit his grandparents or an aunt and uncle. The family only moved from apartment to apartment within the same area when a new baby was born and they outgrew the apartment.[5] Specifically, when the family increased from two to eight children, Bob's father sought out bigger rooms to accommodate two double beds. The family also moved the week after Bob's brother Leo died

The Frenchtown Comb Factory

Robert Cormier created fictional worlds using much of the scenery and setting from his childhood. In *Fade*, he wrote about a young boy, Paul Moreaux, who would grow up to be a writer. Paul lives in the fictional town called Frenchtown, where the men in the family make their livings in a local comb factory. Bob's description of the comb factory depicts his own childhood where his father and uncles toiled in the comb factories of Leominster. Bob's description is an unflinching portrayal of the hardships his relatives endured, complete with walkouts and layoffs and the harshness of working in conditions where fires and injury were everyday fears.

In one scene, Bob describes Paul's descent into the bowels of the comb factory to deliver his father's forgotten lunch to the Rub Room, a room where the rough edges of plastic combs were smoothed over.

"You opened the door of the Rub Room and a blast of purgatory struck your face. The workers sat on stools, huddled like gnomes over the whirling wheels, holding combs against the wheels to smooth away the rough spots. The room roared with the sound of machinery while the foul smell of the mud soiled the air. The mud was a mixture of ashes and water in which the wheels splashed so that they would not overheat at point of contact with the combs. Because the Rub Room was located in the cellar of the shop where there were no windows, the workers toiled in the naked glare of ceiling lights that intensified everything in the room: the noise, the smells, the heat, and the cursing of the men."[5]

because, as he said, they had to leave "those rooms shadowed forever by his death."[7]

Bob attended parochial school and, although his was a family of factory workers, less educated than some, he was encouraged in his love of reading and working with words. He once said, "I can't remember a time I wasn't trying to get something down on paper."[8]

While in seventh grade at St. Cecilia's Grammar School, Bob especially appreciated his seventh grade teacher, Sister Catherine, who was considered "a big boy's nun," and so he wrote her a poem. She read it and announced, "Why, Robert! You are a writer." From that day on, he knew he was a writer.[9]

But Bob was not always so charmed by the examples of his Catholic education. One of his most unhappy memories was of a June day in 1939 when his family home, which he could see from the classroom, burned down. When he rose from his seat to run out and check on the safety of his family, his teacher, made him stop to pray. Although everyone escaped safely, Bob remained angry at that nun for a time.[10]

Despite this memory, Bob recalled a childhood filled with ideal days of heat waves when school was let out because the heat made the classrooms unbearable. "It was too hot to remain in the classroom but never to hot for an afternoon game of Kick the Can or Buck-Buck, How Many Fingers Up in the schoolyard."[11]

Without realizing it, Bob's mother helped him

Bob Cormier was in seventh grade at St. Cecilia's Catholic School (above) when he first discovered his talent for writing.

to become a writer because of a pact she made with God while suffering a serious illness. She vowed that if God helped her regain her health she would always wear blue in devotion to the Blessed Virgin Mary and she would give up the movies. Forever after, she loved to listen to his stories of the Saturday afternoon movies. "I would act out the scenes for her. All around the house, while she was doing her chores. I did a great Bette Davis!"[12]

He wrote later in a column, "She probably had been bored to tears, wondering: Will he ever stop talking?"[13]

His reading interests tended toward short stories such as those found in the very popular *Saturday Evening Post*. He also devoured stories of comic book heroes such as the Green Hornet and Superman.

For his twelfth birthday, Bob's Aunt Victorine gave him the first real book he ever owned, the novel, *The Adventures of Tom Sawyer*. This novel, he said, "pointed out the drama possible in the life of an ordinary boy and thus the potential drama in my own life."[14]

Despite the Depression, the family looked forward to each Christmas celebration. Bob's father would dress as Santa and bring home trees that the family would teasingly pronounce "pathetic."[16] Because his mother loved the color blue, there was

---

"We Didn't Know We Were Poor"

Like so many depression era families, Bob's family worried about keeping their jobs because of layoffs and factory closings. They did without many of the material things that contemporary families take for granted. Writing about that time, he said, "The neighborhood was a poor one by some standards and the Depression was the pollution of our lives. Wednesday was payday, and if your father had worked a full week someone would be sent to the drugstore after supper for those two-for-a-nickel ice-cream cones. We'd sit on the piazza steps—we always called it a piazza, never a porch—and life was suddenly unbearably sweet. The secret, of course, was this: we didn't know we were poor, simply because we didn't know anyone who was rich."[15]

---

a Christmas when Bob saved his money to buy her a set of blue glasses on a silver tray. "It was only many years later that I realized, of course, that in the heart of the Depression I had given her a set of whiskey glasses on a tin tray painted silver, my mother who never held a whiskey glass in her hand. I had seen only the blue that she loved. Looking back now, I realize how much love I was surrounded with, because she pretended, for my sake, that she too, only saw the blue."[17]

Although somewhat of a loner because he was small for his age, Bob had a best friend, Pete Dignard. The two enterprising friends would scour French Hill for empty pop bottles and sell them for two cents each. They also sold soap for a man named "Old Jake" who commissioned them at a penny a sale.

Pete proved himself the best of friends when it came time to play games in groups. "In choosing sides for a game of corner-lot baseball, I was secure in the knowledge that Pete, who was a much better player, would choose me first." Bob, in turn, would allow Pete free admission into the shows he produced in the cellar of his home.[18]

Grade school days transformed to public high school where Bob came into his own and was senior class president and attended proms, recalls his wife, Connie Cormier. "He was very popular with his classmates and teachers."[19]

Connie Senay was two years behind Bob in high school and she and Bob did not actually meet until later. He never even had a class with her. Still she knew of him because he was always in plays and conducted assemblies. "He was a great dancer and talker," she said.[20]

One high school English teacher, E. Lillian Rocker, appreciated Bob's writing talent and often worked with him on his stories after school. He recalled, "I had just discovered similes and metaphors, was drunk on words, and she taught me their proper use. Her blue pencil was lovingly employed."[21]

Although his high school years were untouched by personal tragedy or horror, the world was at war. By the time Bob graduated from high school, the country was thoroughly mired in World War II. It seemed everyone was enlisting to fight and Bob planned to enlist after his graduation. He was terribly disappointed to learn his nearsightedness and low weight would keep him out of the war. "He went to Fort Devens in Nearly Ayer, New Hampshire and tried to enlist two or three times," said Connie, "and was turned down each time because of his eyesight and weight."[22]

Instead of fighting in the war, Cormier prepared for the life of a writer attending Fitchburg State Teacher's College for one year during the day while working at the local factory at night.[23] He perceived obstacles to his chosen career. "My background is very modest," he said, "My father, my uncles and aunts were factory workers or store clerks. I knew no writers, thought you had to be a genius, well educated, must travel the world. And there I was a skinny kid in a three-decker neighborhood, filled with longings and urgings, with few resources."[24] Nevertheless, his parents supported his dream and were proud because he was the first member of his family to attend college.

Cormier often joined his sister Gloria on Saturday evenings to socialize at the local community center. According to biographer Patty Campbell, independent young bachelors like Cormier were popular at the Saturday evening dances. Cormier always saved the first dance for his sister before taking a spin on the floor with her girlfriends. It was at one of these dances that Cormier met petite brunette Connie Senay, born September 28, 1926, who would become his bride. Like Bob, Connie was a French Hill inhabitant, the daughter of a pharmacist. Connie, who worked at the local telephone company, recalled attending the dance with another friend and Bob's sister Gloria.

Campbell recounted Bob's reaction to his dance with Connie: "She was fantastic! We just floated away!" The couple danced the rest of that night's dances together, and soon all the Saturday evening dances became theirs.[25] Connie recalls, "He was a great dancer and talker."[26]

While Cormier was a student at Fitchburg State and dating Connie he made his first professional sale to a Catholic family magazine. One of his teachers, Florence Conlon, typed up and sent one of his short stories, "The Little Things That Count," to *The Sign*. The $75 he earned was his first proof that he could be a writer.[27]

Chapter 3

Small Town Reporter

With the $75 sale of his first short story giving him confidence, Cormier left college to earn his living writing radio commercials for radio station WTAG. The work was challenging for a writer, forcing him to spend words carefully, writing catchy advertisements of 100 or fewer words for the station's sponsors—who could be stern critics.[1]

Despite his disappointment over not being allowed into the armed services, Cormier's life appeared to be charmed. His radio writing job drew the attention of the newspaper that owned the station, the *Worcester Telegram and Gazette*. He was offered a chance to report for the Leominster bureau on the paper's night shift.[2] Bob and Connie celebrated the fulltime reporting job with their marriage on November 6, 1948, a day that Connie remembers as "a gorgeous, warm fall day."[3]

Before long, Bob and Connie had their first child, a daughter named Bobbie, born November 19, 1951. A second child, their son Peter, came along on August 13, 1953. Their third child, another girl named Chris, was born on April 6, 1957. "He was ecstatic!" Connie says of Bob's reaction to the births of each of his children.[4]

Cormier moved up to the *Fitchburg Sentinel and Enterprise* in 1955 where he worked as a reporter and editor.[5] Although his life would appear busy enough with his growing family and reporting, Cormier relied upon the evenings and weekends to pen short stories and begin his first novel.[6]

In an interview with *Kidspace*, an Internet Public Library program, Cormier said his stories were inspired by the news he read and wrote and by his own life. He was always interested in what motivated people to behave in the ways they did. Reporting also made it possible for Cormier to write no matter what his surroundings. "My newspaper years taught me to write amid noise, confusion, phones ringing, people talking, all kinds of interruptions." The writer who began his career picking out letters on the keyboard of a manual typewriter said, "All I need is a typewriter—and time."[7]

Cormier's story ideas sometimes came to him just before he fell asleep. But ideas also came to him while driving his car or while sitting at his typewriter. He said, "The magic virtually happens for me when I'm at the typewriter, writing, the character's developing, the words singing and dancing on the page."[8]

Cormier and Connie's fourth child, Renee, was born on May 15, 1967.[9] About the same time, Cormier began a popular human interest column. He wrote this under the pen name John Fitch IV (after John Fitch who had founded the newspaper), because he believed the pseudonym gave him the freedom to write about personal topics "without embarrassing anyone." The column won the K.R. Thomson newspaper chain's award in 1973.[10]

Renee Cormier Wheeler recalls the significant role writing played in all the family's lives: "Mom created the atmosphere that allowed Dad to write. She always believed in him, even in the early days of their relationship when he was writing short stories.[11] His short stories, the stories he wrote late into the night and on weekends, totaled well over fifty, appearing in the Catholic magazines *The Sign* and the *St. Anthony Messenger*, and also *Scholastic Voice*, *McCall's*, *Woman's Day*, and *Redbook*.[12]

Although he seemed to be constantly writing, he was a strong presence in his children's lives. Renee recalls, "Because I am younger than my siblings by ten or more years and was the only child at home for most of my life, I spent a great deal of time with my father. . . . What strikes me is how available he was to me."[13]

Cormier wrote in at least one column about his love for words and language: "There are certain words I love and use over and over again, words

Robert and Connie Cormier

The *Redbook* Rock Becomes a Family Story

When Cormier sold his first story to *Redbook*, he felt the check was an unexpected gift of riches. He and the family discussed how the money would be spent and, in the end, they decided that Bob should buy his wife a diamond ring because he wanted to purchase a nicer ring than the one he had given her when they became engaged. After the purchase, the family referred to Connie's ring as the *Redbook* rock.[14]

like marvelous and stunning and wonder. . . . I am usually attracted to words by their emotional meanings."[15]

An avid reader, Cormier credited earlier literary influences with shaping his writing. They included Ernest Hemingway, William Saroyan, Thomas Wolfe, J.D. Salinger, and John O'Hara. He particularly admired Graham Greene.[16] He said, "The mentor of my mature years is Graham Greene, the author I try to emulate not imitate. His novels are constant sources of inspiration for me. *The End of the Affair*, one of the great novels of this century, never fails to move me and make me feel like writing. J.D. Salinger and his short stories are writings I turn to all the time. . . . I love detective stories—they always deliver a beginning, middle and end, a satisfying climax or epiphany."[17]

The Day of the Jackal was one novel he even

discussed in one of his columns. "Absolutely first rate storytelling," he wrote. "That ancient art so often neglected by some of the so-called literary writers, who are too busy being cute and cunning with symbolism and metaphor to engage us with the pace that thrills."[18]

But he also loved music and movies, with particular favorites and concerns becoming the topic of columns. In a column entitled, "Does the Melody Linger On?" he wrote of the way melodies could captivate him so that he would play them over and over and over again: "I am enchanted by 'Without You,' for instance, a heart-wrenching song delivered by Nilsson, and it plays and plays, repeating its loveliness on the stereo into the small hours of the night. And I think: I'll love this song forever. I will be playing this years from now. And then it begins to pall."[19]

He told readers that he wondered if he should see *The Exorcist*. It was not because he feared the topic of exorcism. On the contrary, horror movies were a particular favorite. But Cormier had read the book. In fact, could not put it down. He worried that the movie would fail to live up to the novel.[20]

While Cormier's life was full of small and thoughtful moments, such as those captured in his early columns, moments that made for a rich and family-oriented life, his close-knit family also experienced times of grief. Heart-stricken when he learned his father was suffering from terminal cancer, he and his siblings could not talk about his

Starting Together

With the sale of Cormier's first novel, Marilyn Marlow, who became a renowned author's agent, began Cormier's writing career with him. She said, "*Now and at the Hour* was the first novel he published and the first novel that I as a beginning agent ever sold. From my viewpoint, it was a wonderful relationship—42 years of admiration on my part and a special friendship with a gentle, kind, generous and always complex man." [21]

father's impending death. Instead Cormier wrote about the experience.

His first novel, an adult novel, *Now and at the Hour,* depicts the steady progression of cancer in a man's life when he is stripped each day of a little more dignity, his energy, the ability to work, and finally his life. The novel, published in 1960, was, in reality, a fictionalized account of his father's death. [22]

With the support of his agent, Marilyn E. Marlow of Curtis Brown, Ltd., Cormier published his two other adult novels *A Little Raw on Monday Mornings* in 1963, and *Take Me Where the Good Times Are* in 1965, before the advent of *The Chocolate War*, the novel that gave him the opportunity to focus on his new audience, young adult readers. [23]

Chapter 4

The Chocolate War and Beyond

While readers and critics alike recognized that the stark language in *The Chocolate War* captured the reality of boys in a private school, they were also aware that it contained sexually honest references and a gloomy ending depicting evil that is allowed to flourish. His fans praised the novel for breaking new ground in young adult literature. But, when it came out, *Booklist* ran a review surrounded by a black border that accused Cormier of corrupting America's youth.[1]

Despite the controversy, the aftermath of the book's success provided Cormier the dream of a lifetime to write fiction full time. Connie remained at the telephone company, taking advantage of the benefits and pension. Cormier agreed to continue his columns from home. But now he worked at the typewriter in his dining room office each and every day.[2]

With his new schedule, Bobbie, Peter and Chris, Cormier's three oldest children, would arrive home from school to a dad who, during a break from writing, had begun the evening meal. "I would get home at 2:30 and he would be making meatloaf," recalls Chris. "I'd help him peel potatoes. But I never realized then how unusual it was to have my dad there."[3]

Cormier never acted as though life should be any different either. The prolific writer took everything in stride, saying, "It's wonderful that people are writing about me and calling *The Chocolate War* a classic, but I'm still a working writer who faces the blank page every day."[4]

Cormier settled into the routine of typing out his imaginative journeys inside the world of young adults on his old manual typewriter. Challenges questioned the inclusion of his book on school and community library shelves because some perceived its message—to take a stand alone can lead to violence and potential demise—was overly negative. But many of Cormier's teen readers, teachers, and librarians loved the book for its honesty. The novel posed a real and serious dilemma when it asked, "Should you stand up for your beliefs if it means suffering?"[5]

One young fan explained, "People in the world don't like individuals."[6]

Another fan said that *The Chocolate War* captured the way cliques are valued over individuals

When Your Father Is a Writer

Renee Cormier Wheeler was ten years old when her father left the newspaper to write full time at home. So Renee was usually with her dad after school and on vacations. He never had an office door to close off from any of his children. Renee recalls that he was almost always available to her. When she accompanied him on errands and trips to the library, she recalls, "Sometimes I had the sense that his mind was far away with his books, `plotting´, as he used to call it, but often we had wonderful conversations about his childhood memories, my hopes and dreams, books, movies . . . pretty much everything."

Sixth grade was a particularly difficult year for Renee, who said that, although she had one friend, she did not seem to have much status with her peers. It was as if the rest of the girls in class had gotten together without her, "to decide that boys and clothes were more interesting than horses." She felt left out and unhappy. Sunday nights she'd sit with her father in his recliner thinking about how badly she did not want to go to school on Monday. Her father seemed to understand. She recalls that he once said, "You know, one or two true friends are all you really need in this world. You don't need to be the most popular girl in school. Just a couple of real friends and you're doing just fine."[7]

in the high school world. "To us, it's big and it's real . . . [Cormier] seems to relate to that," said a high school junior, quoted in her local newspaper after Cormier made an appearance at her school in 1974.[8]

At this time, Cormier was in the thick of writing his second young adult novel, a psychological thriller, *I Am the Cheese.* As he sat at his typewriter, creating a fictional world in which a character named Adam races on a bike to aid his father, he felt the thrill of writing. He came to see clearly that "adolescence is not the lighthearted Betty-and-Veronica world that many adults paint it to be." When he compared what he wrote to his own adolescence, he recalled that it had its horrible moments as well.[9]

In his writing, he became all the people he wanted to be. He saw himself as an entertainer, telling audiences, "Whenever something terrible happens to me, I say 'Maybe I can use it in a story.' That's why I'll never get ulcers."[10]

Cormier's writing was guided by the emotion of daily events in the lives of all the people around him. He began to realize that his heart ached to be with young adults. "I find I write more dramatically when I put young people in my stories," he once told a teen audience. "Writing about adults is dull, but young people are so dramatic, they go through every type of emotion in a day."[11]

In writing, he saw clearly that inspiration came out of his life experience. He could use any incident or emotion and create fiction out of it. Everything

Spreading the Message
to Start Writing

On school visits, Cormier made it his goal to encourage would-be writers in his audiences. His message was clear: Start writing now. "Write daily; keep a journal; pretend you are writing a letter. The thing to do is get something down on paper. Then you can always correct it, rewrite it, polish it."

He would tell teens that writing regularly was more important than having talent. "I know a lot of talented people," Cormier said. "But they never get to a typewriter."

"If I could have met a writer when I was a young person and found him to be human, it would have been easier for me (to believe I could be a writer)." He added, "Now I'm a writer, but I'm also an ordinary person."[12]

that happened to him seemed to be the stuff of drama.

When he was writing, his characters would take over. Then things might happen to his characters that he did not expect. Sometimes he would end his writing day leaving things up in the air, and he realized that in life you do not always have the answers either. But each morning he returned to his typewriter and his chair. "The only extraordinary thing about me," he once said, "is that I sit at the typewriter day after day and write. If I

Cormier playing the piano.

spend a day at home and don't write anything, I feel like I've committed a sin."[13]

While writing *I Am the Cheese*, Cormier spent five to six hours each day writing about Adam, who begins his journey in that fictitious town called Monument, the town that so strongly resembles his own Leominster.

Sometimes, when he would take a break, perhaps to pick up groceries at the Victory Market, he would find the best idea of the day would come to him and he realized that ordinary settings could

---

Phone Home

There is a scene in *I Am the Cheese* in which Adam tries to phone his friend, Amy. She is his only connection to the normal life of his past, his only tie to reality.

Cormier, a stickler for realism, did not like the idea of using a fictitious 555 code for the first three local digits and so he inserted his own home number into the text of his manuscript. After the novel came out, and grew in popularity, so did phone calls to his home asking for Amy Hertz.

Young readers were surprised when the author answered calls and sometimes even played along with them, indicating he was Amy's father.

He would answer their questions about the novel before hanging up. Cormier said that in all the years that the calls came in, he never once received a late night phone call from pranksters.[14]

---

stimulate his imagination. He knew, too, that he was not writing to make people feel good. He was writing to upset people. He once said, "The worst thing in the world is indifference."[15]

Even as the writing of his second young adult novel drew to a close, Cormier's first novel continued to come under fire. Cormier must have enjoyed the irony that, despite this, *The Chocolate War* continued to be recommended more than any other young adult novel, according to the American Library Association.[16]

Chapter 5

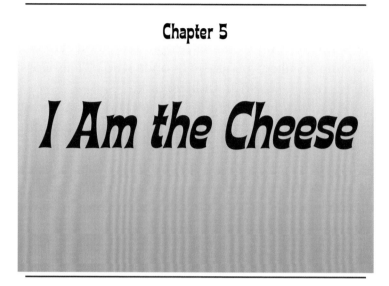

I Am the Cheese

When *I Am the Cheese* was published, the novel raised as many questions as it answered. Cormier said he had intentionally made this novel an ambiguous work. He wanted his readers to be so closely inside his main character Adam's head that the reader would have trouble distinguishing reality from paranoia. The fast-paced novel, told in three voices—Adam's; the interrogator, who is in reality a psychiatrist named Brint; and an omniscient narrator—develops a collage of mysteries and secrets.[1]

But this is no ordinary mystery. *I Am the Cheese* is a psychological thriller that intentionally disorients and confuses first-time readers, making them think like the paranoid they believe Adam to be.[2] The plot pits teen-aged Adam against a world controlled by large institutions and corrupt governments in a way that makes the reader share Adam's predicament in not knowing who he can trust. Readers recognize the dilemma of humanity versus the system, and "the cruelty of life and its injustice at permitting the innocent to suffer and the evil to prosper."[3] A *Horn Book Magazine* reviewer, Paul Heins, said, "Mr. Cormier is actually writing about human integrity; and in the course of doing so, he cogently uncovers the lacerations that evil often inflicts upon the innocent."[4]

The novel opens with Adam frantically pedaling his bike to Vermont to visit his hospitalized father after the two have narrowly escaped capture by members of a secret agency. Readers slowly discover that much of what occurs is in Adam's mind.[5]

Readers of all ages have admired the novelist's craftsmanship since it was published. Cormier's stories, with their surprising twists and turns, came from living in a world of four growing children, whose adolescent problems seemed so real and traumatic to him when he watched the world through their eyes. Like Adam, they were "individuals being dehumanized by the large institutions of society."[6]

Cormier knew that he had struck a connection with the young adult age group with *I Am the Cheese* when a University of Massachusetts student said that to see Adam so alone in the world gave her some comfort in her own loneliness.[7]

Interviewers could not help contrasting the

mild-mannered family man to the author recognized for writing yet another uncompromising young adult novel with a grim ending. There was a certain incongruity to it all.[8]

Cormier explained, "I want to hit the reader with whatever emotion I want to portray, or whatever action that will make it vivid. . . . I want the reader to *feel* the emotion of the characters. And I would use any word, any unpretty image, to communicate that emotion. So this is what I aim for: clarity. I feel good when someone says to me: 'I know exactly what you meant.'"[9]

One of the most exciting moments of Cormier's life occurred when Hollywood came calling. "He was vibrating when he got off the phone," said Connie, who was at home when Bob learned that *I Am the Cheese* had been optioned as a movie which would be scheduled for 1983 release.

Cormier's love of movies intertwined with his writing when he took his family on location to Vermont to see the bicycle riding scenes played out. Cormier himself played a small role in the film. He was "enthralled" to be in the Hollywood environment, says Connie. One day while Bob was watching filming, Robert Wagner, the handsome, popular actor who played young Adam's psychiatrist, embraced Bob to demonstrate how he wanted to change a scene. Wagner believed the scene would benefit if he wrestled with Adam. "Cormier's reaction had nothing to do with the film," said a reporter who talked to Cormier just

While working as a columnist and editor, Cormier spent evenings and weekends at the typewriter writing novels and short stories in a small office off the dining room of his home.

after this. "Instead he wondered how many women wished they were in his shoes."

Back at home, the writer returned to work on his next young adult novel. His wife, Connie, was editing a collection of her husband's columns scheduled for spring publication. When Cormier contemplated his luck and his dreams, he said, "You don't have to travel the Seven Seas, you can find it [luck] right in your home town."[10]

He told an audience that as a child, while watching movies on Saturday afternoons, he had dreamed of being Humphrey Bogart. He felt that, when *I Am the Cheese* had been made into a movie, that dream became reality when he played the role of a newspaper editor. "This scrawny kid from French Hill was in a movie. Don't tell me dreams don't come true." But the self-deprecating author admitted to his audience that during the Leominster premiere, it became apparent when he saw himself on the twelve foot screen that he was no Humphrey Bogart.

After leaving that group, he received a note from one of the students. "You're Humphrey Bogart in your own way," the note said.[11]

FAQs for *I Am the Cheese*

Many readers came away from *I Am the Cheese* with unanswered questions. They wrote so frequently to Cormier that graduate students at Fitchburg State College created this FAQ sheet to be mailed out in response to them. Cormier made sure that the answers were still vague enough not to give anything away.[12]

1. Who is Brint? Is he a government agent trying to help Adam regain his mental health, or is he an enemy trying to retrieve secret information from Adam's subconscious?

Brint is "T" on the tapes. "T" being the last letter of his name. I wanted the reader to be jolted by "T: Good morning. My name is Brint." The reader immediately knows that something's up—things are not what they seem. Brint is a government agent trying to retrieve any information or knowledge Adam has about his father's past, or about the "accident" that killed his parents. He is simply an employee of the department, doing his job, but also evil. Evil is sometimes very commonplace. Thousands of Nazis who killed millions of Jews contended they were only doing their job, taking and following orders.

2. Who runs the hospital where Adam is being questioned?

The hospital is operated by the government. The people in the hospital were also patients; not all were victims, perhaps of the agency. The agency might have been using a legitimate hospital as a front for the few "patients" of their own. The questioning of Adam was necessary because of the rules of the agency. However, they did not know how much Adam had been told by his father, and there was a small chance Adam had information no one else had.

3. What will become of Adam? Will he regain his memory? Will the doctors at this hospital kill him? Or will he stay at the hospital until he dies?

I think that Adam/Paul is still at the hospital bicycling around and managing to hold on. I keep hoping that he hasn't been terminated, and that perhaps someday he will be rescued or will get away.

4. Who was responsible for the deaths of Adam's mother and father? Did their own government agent turn on them, or did the "Syndicate" eliminate them?

The farmers were killed by the Syndicate. Adam's father either died as a result of the crash, or got away for a short time, but was eventually killed by the Syndicate. The important thing for Adam is that he did not see his father actually die. Grey/Thompson, the government agent, fingered the family for the Syndicate, perhaps yielding to pressure from both sides to get rid of the farmers.

5. What part did Grey/Thompson play in their deaths? Was he a double agent?

Grey was not part of the Syndicate. He was not a double agent in the usual sense, although he double-crossed Adam's father, setting him up for the Syndicate and the accident. He was present at the scene to clean up afterward, but hadn't counted on Adam's survival—an embarrassment to the agency. He embodies the amorality of agencies and syndicates and others when they are entities unto themselves, an example of absolute power corrupting absolutely.

6. Did Amy really exist in Adam's past, or was she a figment of his imagination?

Amy was real. I introduced her into the story as a device to give poor Adam a little comfort and romance, and also to brighten up the story for the reader. She was not part of any plot or sinister event.

7. What happened to Amy in the story? Why did she just disappear? Was she part of the conspiracy?

Her family simply moved out of town. As it often happens in real life, you meet people and they move away. Remember, there are three years between the time of the murder of the parents and Adam/Paul's questioning by Brint in the novel. Amy was completely innocent and not part of the conspiracy.

8. How much of Adam's bike trip to see his father was real, and how much was fantasy?

Adam/Paul, traumatized by his parents' death, and drugged by doctors at the hospital, goes on a fantasy bicycle trip. Because Adam did not see his father die, he thought he was still alive, and was searching for him in his fantasy ride around the grounds of the institution.

9. Why did you use the tape recordings in the novel, and why are they designated OZK?

A lot of readers ask this question. The tape recordings were used in order to bring to the reader a great deal of material in simplified form (otherwise the novel would have been too long and cumbersome). The tape designations OZK001, etc., are meant as this clue: OZ stands for OZ as in "The Wizard of . . ." Dorothy, after the tornado, meets in fantasy, the real like people she knew in town. That's what happened to Adam/Paul as he bicycled around the grounds of the institution in his trauma.

10. Where did you get the idea or motivation for this story? Is it based on a real incident, or on someone you know?

The boy Adam is patterned after me as a boy, the first time I've written anything autobiographical in my novels. I was shy, wanted to be a writer, was often chased by dogs on my newspaper route, and was intimidated by bullies. I get my ideas observing what's going on in the world, reading (both books and newspapers) and trying to figure what would happen if these events happened to ordinary people like Adam. But the other events are fiction, based on research, of course. My motivation for writing this story was to explore the dangers of government invading people's privacy; to show how good concepts of government can be trashed by corrupt men; and to point out that in today's world it's hard to tell the good guys from the bad. I also wanted to show the complex, threatening world we live in today, a world in which we never have all the answers to what's going on around us.

11. Could you explain the obscure ending of the novel?

Although there is some ambiguity involved in the ending, most of the answers can be found in a careful reading, especially the chapter which deals with tape OZK016. If that chapter is read carefully, matching numbers to people, and if motivations are checked out (regarding #2222 especially), the storyline should emerge. I wanted to make the novel lifelike, and life doesn't always provide all the answers or a happy ending for us.

---

12. Will you write a sequel to *I AM THE CHEESE?*

I am not contemplating a sequel at the moment, but who knows?[13]

I Am the Cheese won the Phoenix Award, awarded for a book originally published in English which did not receive a major award upon publication, in 1997. That same year Fitchburg State College awarded the author an Honorary Doctorate of Letters in recognition of excellence in writing.[14]

With the publication of his next novel, *The Bumblebee Flies Anyway* in 1983, Cormier solidified his reputation as a master of psychological stories that carry a message to beware of large institutions. This novel, about terminally ill patients being used as involuntary guinea pigs in an experimental hospital, raises "some profound questions about medical ethics, about manipulation and about the attitudes of the dying and those closest to them." While the style of writing was described as "merciless," reviewers saw some hope in the end where Cormier captured a "mood of magnificent optimism . . . soaring from the terrible mundanity of pain and suffering to the inspiring and poetic victory of the unbroken human spirit."[15]

It was not just the realism that held his readers. They relished the fast-moving scenes and spare dialogue. The apparently simple stories with intricate structures and layer upon layer of meaning, created an intense emotional element, "a dark awareness of evil as an implacable obstacle."[16]

With his previous novels gaining more and more acclaim, and almost a decade after writing *The Chocolate War*, Cormier began work on a long-awaited sequel, *Beyond the Chocolate War*. Fans had constantly asked him if Jerry had survived and what happened to the Vigil leader, Archie. Cormier himself admitted the original novel's outcome captured his imagination. He, too, had questions about the characters, especially Obie, with whom he identified more than any other character.[17] Were these characters to succumb to the typical Cormier fate?

As he sat at his typewriter, Cormier must have wondered if his protagonists would be his usual tragic heroes losing out to evil. He must have asked himself if the sequel would reflect the world's reality as he saw it, a place where evil operates.[18]

Chapter 6

Censorship and Challenges

*E*veryday after *The Chocolate War* had found its way into classrooms, Cormier was conscious that his novels were the focus of challenges and attempted bans. The first really serious challenge to this book—from Groton, Massachusetts, a city close to his home—came in 1982 when the book was criticized for being too negative. Critics in Lapeer, Michigan attempted to challenge the book shortly thereafter. It also came under attack in Irmo, North Carolina and in Proctor, Vermont, where the school board decided against banning the book by only one vote.[1]

In 1984, *The Chocolate War* had been removed from the Richland, South Carolina schools' middle school shelves and placed on optional reading lists for the high schools because of "pervasive vulgarity."

"It does use strong language," he admitted. But he argued that the language was less harsh than what might be heard in school halls or on school buses. "The thing that bothers me about the entire thing," he lamented, "is that they [the censors] are reading the words and not the meaning." Cormier was concerned too, that his message in *The Chocolate War*, that the system breaks down when good people fail to take action, would be overlooked now by readers who were only looking for the language censors had attacked.[2]

"I admit it is a strong book," Cormier said. "But I think a strong book is needed these days to get an essential message across."[3]

He was immeasurably grateful to the teachers and librarians who supported his work and the rights of students to read and discuss the challenging topics his work presented, and felt an obligation to support the teachers in their efforts. So even as Cormier worked on the sequel to *The Chocolate War,* his writing time became divided by the need to defend his work, especially his first young adult novel, against increasingly frequent challenges.

Each attack felt like a personal affront to Cormier, who defended himself by saying, "I wrote with integrity and I try to write with a moral theme."[4]

In an essay he wrote for The Children's Book Council defending *The Chocolate War*, Cormier said he had written his young adult novels out of "complete innocence," "without thinking of marketing or labels." He pointed out that advance reviews of

The Chocolate War had warned the book would bring on controversy because it came out in a time when YA novels "did not tackle controversial issues."

But Cormier said, if attempts to censor and ban his book had been effective, the book would not have won awards, it would not continue to be taught in classrooms 25 years after its appearance, and it would not have been translated into at least a dozen languages or reissued as an anniversary edition in hardback.[5]

"I like to think, perhaps immodestly, that the novel has survived because it rings with the truth, that it explores and does not exploit," Cormier

Robert Cormier and his family on the set of *I Am The Cheese*. (Shown from left to right: Cormier, Robert McNaughton who played Adam Farmer, Cormier's wife Connie, Bobbi, Renee, Peter and Chris.)

wrote. He knew that it was a difficult book for some readers. Sensitive young people might find aspects of the novel unsettling and possibly objectionable. Some teachers would find it impossible to teach. Parents leafing through the pages without reading the complete book would be upset by certain words or descriptions. But Cormier had also received letters from countless readers who found this novel valuable. "Through the years," he wrote, "I have received countless letters from young people who say that the novel helped them through their adolescent years, that the novel was the first that spoke to them truthfully, 'told it like it is,' confirmed to them what they already knew but seldom encountered in other school-assigned books—that life does not guarantee happy endings. And they have thanked me for writing it."[6]

When *Beyond the Chocolate War* made its debut in 1985, it, too, promised to be a controversial novel. Reviewers recognized "its uncompromising view of human weaknesses, as well as its honest depiction of the language and personalities of male high school students." These same reviewers promised this would be another young adult best seller for the same reasons.[7]

Toward the mid-1980s, Cormier noticed a shift in the way challenges occurred. Groups that claimed his books did not belong in the schools or even in the hands of his readers seemed more organized and aggressive in their attempts to remove the work of other respected authors and his own work from library and school shelves.

Censors no longer limited attacks to *The Chocolate War*. Now *I Am the Cheese* was being called into question. He grew increasingly concerned about the effect these censors had on his fellow authors who were beginning to write cautiously.[8]

In defense of writers, he said, "words that go into books are not chosen gratuitously or casually."[9]

Cormier understood the motivation of many of his censors. "It is the act of sincere, sometimes desperate people who are frightened by the world they live in and in which they are bringing up their children. They are trying to do the impossible, to shield their children from this world, to control what they see and do, what they learn."[10]

But in Cormier's eyes, each challenge changed the climate for writers and readers and cut into their freedom. "In each of these cases," he said, "they are always limiting access in some way,

---

Who Can Quarrel with Well-Meaning Parents?

Cormier understood the parents who felt they were protecting their children. He, himself, omitted a chapter from publication in *The Chocolate War* because, when his fifteen-year old daughter Chris had asked to read the manuscript, he had found himself uncomfortable with the sexually explicit scene it depicted. That scene was cut and has never been read by anyone but Cormier's editor.[11]

---

putting a compromise on the book. And every time you compromise, you're giving up part of your freedom."[12]

While Cormier argued for parents' rights to protect their children, he also understood that sometimes the very motivation to protect could make a parent to go too far. "At the moment when their children are reaching out beyond the boundaries of home and family, they are raising the barriers to that reaching out. Instead of preparing them to meet that world, they want them to avert their eyes and remain in impossible exclusion."[13]

What truly offended Cormier's sensibility was the way these parents used censorship to reach beyond their own families when they insisted, by limiting a book's distribution, that the same sheltering be extended to people who might live next door, down the street or in the next town.[14]

Cormier repeated again and again that offensive words were sometimes necessary to accurately portray contemporary characters. "It's when people read out of context that there's a problem," he said in 1985. "Kids don't go around saying 'golly gee.' Anyone who's been on a school bus knows that. You have to write realistically." He added, "It is the death of creativity when you sit at a typewriter and are afraid to say things. I know I am writing in conservative times but I need to write honestly."[15]

Despite his efforts, censorship of Cormier's books continued in subtle ways. Cormier lamented the climate for publishing, saying, "We are now in

Controversy Does Not Come from Those Who Read His Books

It irritated Cormier greatly that the majority of complaints and challenges to his books came, not from his teen readers, but from parents and members of the community who felt they needed to protect kids from the harsh realities of life. "The controversy doesn't come from kids," he said. "They would like, but understand they can't always have, a happy ending. They can absorb more than most think."[16]

a more conservative era, censorship attempts are virtually a daily occurrence."[17]

His personal challenge in this climate was to continue "bringing these characters to life. "Striving for clarity so that each event in a novel was sharp and clear as that crystal scene under glass just before you shake it and the snowflakes fall."[18]

Cormier talked of the censorship battle that had occurred in Vermont. A librarian there fought to keep *The Chocolate War* on the shelves. After weeks of arguments and attacks, the school board voted to support the novel. She called Cormier and reported the win. As jubilant as she was, Cormier saw the victory as only a small gain. The vote had been three to two and the novel was given special status with limitations on who could read it attached to its return to the shelves.

"Despite all this," he said. "We must continue the fight. Writers depend on courageous people like that librarian in Vermont to continue the day-to-day skirmishing with would-be censors."[19]

In 1985, a string of six teen suicides in his own community reaffirmed Cormier's belief that there was a real need for books like his, books that spoke to young adults about what was really happening in their lives. "Now they know these things are going on in the world. Why try to hide them. . . . Is it better to hide it or is it better to try to explain motives and to realize these things happen? I simply could not sit down and write any novel thinking it might upset the sensibilities of a fourteen year old boy or girl. That would be the death of all creativity for me."[20]

In the end, he did not feel he should have to defend his books at all. "I wrote it, period," he said. "If someone doesn't like it, that's their problem. I let the book speak for itself."[21]

Meanwhile, *The Chocolate War* had been made into a film that was released on October 28, 1988 in Los Angeles and New York as a benefit for Amnesty International.[22]

Cormier's next novel, *Fade*, published 1988, proved that he was not a man to give in to censorship and write what would appeal to those who sought to remove his books from the shelves. In this novel, the main character, 13-year-old Paul Moreaux, discovers that he can make himself invisible. It is a study of the way power can corrupt an individual. Paul witnesses illegal and immoral acts and must decide if he will use his ability to fade and become invisible for good or evil.[23]

Cormier was ready for the censors this time. He readily defended the study of good versus evil in his work, describing the effect of burying evil out of fear that to acknowledge it can make people themselves evil: "It's people who deny evil that there's no hope for. Once you know about the existence of evil, then you can start to fight it. Evil doesn't come out of a cave at night—it wears the bland face of the man who belongs to the Rotary Club, or the grocer."[24]

Chapter 7

Secrets of Everyday Heroes

Set during World War II, Cormier's next novel, *Other Bells for Us to Ring*, which came out in 1990, continued to explore more subtle aspects of good vs. evil in the tension between two girls and their very different religions.[1]

That novel was followed in 1991 by *We All Fall Down*, about a teen who calls himself the Avenger. He witnesses a group of peers trash the house of a girl he cares for and then assault and seriously injure her sister. This novel of secrets and revenge demonstrates Cormier's interest in individual integrity. He explores the isolating consequences of choosing to take a stand alone when doing the honorable thing.[2]

Bob encouraged Connie and all four children to read his finished manuscripts and make editorial

Did He Ever Get Angry?

The irony about Cormier's personality is that, while he was always the mild mannered and humorous father at home, his novels revealed dark and unforgiving aspects of life. His family believes this is an outcome of all his newspaper years when he covered the daily conflicts and tragedies of his city.

Cormier had a long fuse and was generally even tempered. All three daughters do recall one April Fools day when he did become irate once after they hid his typewriter and he could not write.

Renee also recalls that when she was little, her older siblings Chris and Peter would roughhouse by pushing her between them like a football. Then her father, who might be at the typewriter or beginning the family supper, would holler up the stairs, "Ren! Get down here!"

She says, even then he was not really angry. "He was afraid they were going to hurt me."[3]

comments. "If we said something that his editor had said, he would consider it," his daughter Chris recalls of those readings. "He really embraced the age of adolescence and teenage-hood. He really got it."[4]

Bobbie, adds, "He revisited it [adolescence] over and over again. He constantly revisited both the good and the bad."[5]

Tunes for Bears to Dance To, published in

Cormier discusses his work with some teenage fans in a school library.

1992, studies the consequences of choosing to ignore evil. This is a story of a lonely teenager named Henry who is befriended at his grocery store job by the owner. The bigoted grocer attempts to draw Henry into an act of terrible cruelty against a neighbor who is a Holocaust survivor.[6] "The sin is to do nothing," Cormier explained.[7]

Just as in *Fade* and *We All Fall Down*, this novel focuses on the price people pay to hide their secret selves from the rest of the world. Cormier considered his own secrets, and the duality of his identity. "Look at me," he wrote. "I cry at sad movies, long for happy endings, delight in atrocious puns,

Sitting at the Writing Desk

In a 1998 interview with Patty Campbell, Cormier described his writing space for Amazon readers. "I sit here at my old LC Smith typewriter and look over the water. It's very quiet—they don't allow motorboats or water-skiing or anything—and I have a blue heron that often sits there at the edge of the pond waiting patiently, and then all of a sudden spears a fish and then moves on a little ways and waits for another one. Just to the left is a small island—and there's something mysterious about that island, you know. Our deck goes right to the water's edge—look, a little chipmunk just ran across the deck. It's a nice setting, and I always have a good summer of writing here."[8]

He did not mention in that interview that there was still no door to close off his writing space because he wanted his family always to feel welcome to come in and talk. Chris, Renee, and Bobbie recall that, although he was always ready to listen, there were times he sent them on errands, usually to the local grocery store, a good forty-five minute trek, to fetch a pack of cigarettes or supper ingredients. They were grown up when they realized this was his way of getting additional writing time.[9]

pause to gather branches of bittersweet at the side of the highway. I am shamelessly sentimental—I always make a wish when I blow out the candles on my birthday cake, and I dread the day when there may be no one there to say 'Bless you' when I sneeze. Although I aspire to be Superman, I am doomed to be Clark Kent forever, in an endless search for that magic telephone booth. I wear a trench coat, but nobody ever mistakes me for Humphrey Bogart. I hesitate to kill a fly, but people die horrible deaths in my novels."[10]

Patty Campbell, who became a friend when she worked on an early biography of the writer, once told Cormier that she sees themes of concealed identity and invisibility in many of his works. He responded, "I really believe that most people hide who they really are, and I think we all have hidden lives. In fact, one of the things I like about the Internet is that I get on there, and I know I'm in disguise."[11]

Cormier's next book, *In the Middle of the Night*, published in 1995, clearly contains the theme of hidden identities. This novel tells of an adolescent's efforts to learn why his family receives mysterious late night phone calls that lead to frequent moves. Denny Colbert slowly unravels that his father is keeping a secret from him. Denny discovers that his father, as a young man, might have been responsible for a tragic accident that killed 22 children when a movie theatre's roof caved in. While Denny's father has tried to put the memory into the past, the victims' families stalk his family.[12]

Chapter 8

Cormier's Readers Change Over Time

By the late 1990s Cormier recognized changes in his audience. He felt they were more idealistic than he himself had been, although he sometimes worried that they might squander their ideals. "I trust the kids," he finally decided. "I have always been involved with my own children as well as their friends, and I'm pleased with what I see. I am also impressed with the enthusiastic students to whom I've spoken at junior and senior high schools. The future rests with them."[1]

And so he continued to write books that would make his audiences think.

In discussing all of his work, Cormier also said that he relied on his own memories of adolescence to capture the emotions of his characters. If any of his novels was a love story, he believed it was *We*

Their Father Is Their Hero

Cormier's adult children recall their father as an everyday hero because of his gentle nature. They mentioned not only his sense of humor, but his love of fast food, and his even-tempered nature. He was their hero because of the way he remained steadfastly involved with his family. Even as his books gained more popularity, came under closer scrutiny and gathered attention from all the corners of the world, being translated into a number of languages, his family came first. While he traveled more frequently, he took Connie and his youngest daughter, Renee with him.[2]

All Fall Down. He admitted that he had felt much apprehension at writing this because he was relying upon his own memory of what adolescent love could be like. "I know today's kids are supposed to have a lot of knowledge about sex, but I think there's still a kind of an innocence there. When a boy and girl get together, they're still fumbling. "[3] Even though Cormier followed his instincts, when he finished, he worried if the love story worked. He was relieved to learn through letters from readers that he had succeeded. "I got a letter from a girl about that last scene, where they part. She says, 'I read it over and over and it still breaks my heart. I want it so much to not be that way, and I'm always drawn to it.' I had some letters saying they wished that Buddy and Jane had gotten together, but they knew." Cormier claimed their young love was doomed from the beginning.[4]

His work continued to reflect his own fear that young adults might fail to do the right thing in the struggle to respond positively to evil. *Tenderness*, published in 1997, proved to be one of his most provocative works in this regard, when he confronted ultimate depravity. It is the story of an 18-year-old serial killer; Lori a 15-year-old runaway who obsesses over him; and "an old cop who suspects more than he can prove." In this novel, Cormier explored the darkest aspects of tenderness, based upon a theory put forth by Kahil Gibran that there is pain in too much tenderness. "At the time," he explained, "I was also reading in the papers about a lot of instances in which young offenders would be sent to a youth service place instead of jail, and then released at the age of 21, no matter what the crime." Cormier returned to the one question that set off all of his plots, What if?[5]

In the novel, Lori pursues the serial killer, despite warnings, believing that he can love her tenderly.[6]

While this novel's topic dealt with victimization and depravity, Cormier noted that his youngest readers were writing about more mature themes and frightening changes in their own worlds. "There is a difference in that the 11-year old writing to me today sounds like the 16-year old kid of twenty years ago. My readers are getting younger; I get letters now from fifth and sixth graders."[7]

The theme of guilt plays into some of Cormier's later works, especially *Heroes*, published in 1998. In this novel, Frances Cassevant, who has lost his face because of an act of betrayal by his childhood hero, returns from World War II with the goal of finding and killing his childhood hero.[8] Cormier said, "I think our lives are driven by guilt. . . . God is always there to forgive you, but it's harder forgiving yourself."[9]

He tried to define true heroism in this tragic novel. He said, "The impetus came from two areas—the 50th anniversary of D-day, which recalled those war years, and the obituaries in the local paper of men and women who had fought World War II, telling of what they did in that war, stuff that surprised me even with people I had

Years after his death, Cormier's office remains as it was and his novels remain on the American Library Association's list of the ten most banned books.

known." His heroes were the ordinary people who performed their duties without drawing attention to themselves. "I feel that we're surrounded by heroes and saints in our daily lives," he said. "My father worked 44 years in the shops, provided for his family, even in the hard times. When he died, I realized that he would have given up his life for me."[10]

By now in his seventies and despite a fall down some stairs in which he broke his back in 1997, Cormier continued to write, to travel the world, and to speak out against censorship and encourage readers and other writers.

While Cormier continued to work on his novels, he also volunteered to write the history of St. Cecilia's Church, where he had been baptized, across the street from the school where he had witnessed his burning house. This was the church in which he married Connie, and attended his entire life. Connie typed revisions for him on the computer but he still worked on his typewriter, only using the computer for email.[11]

Frenchtown Summer, a novel in poetry, was released in 1999, introducing a more sensitive, side of Cormier.[12] This poetic, almost autobiographical novel, again set in Monument, told the story of a young paperboy's growing awareness of a murder on the streets of his town. According to Cormier, there really was a murder that traumatized him as a boy in the town where he ended up living his entire life.[13]

It was this murder that may have helped him

A Visit to a Juvenile Detention Center

In November 1997, Cormier attended a class of juvenile offenders at the Judge J. Connelly Youth Service Center near Boston as a writer for the PEN Readers & Writers Program, a program that sends writers to areas with limited access to literary culture. He worried that these incarcerated readers might notice inaccuracies in his descriptions of a juvenile detention center. The students were initially standoffish, believing he would be "a rich old white man." Cormier broke through their icy reserve when he entered, appearing frail and carrying two pillows for his back, but easing everyone into a comfortable discussion when he said honestly that the character Lori was based upon an alluring classmate from his own high school years. "Once the questions start, and you answer the first couple very honestly, without lecturing, it opens up," Cormier said.[14]

The students let Cormier know that, while he captured the emotional feeling of a detention facility, many were put off by the downbeat ending and sympathetic portrayal of a serial killer. Cormier said if he had any message in this book, it was that people are all alike. Deep down, everyone is weak. "We're all looking for a little tenderness."[15]

realize that, in novels, "There are no taboos. Every topic is open, however shocking. It is the way that the topics are handled that's important, and that applies whether it is a 15-year-old who is reading your book or someone who is 55."[16]

Ironically, while Cormier often felt the topics in *Tenderness* required defending in front of audiences, he still most often had to defend *The Chocolate War* from censorship. During a challenge of the novel in Lancaster, Massachusetts, in January 2000, Cormier told a reporter with the Associated Press, "I do get tired of it. I wrote the book. In a way I feel, 'Why should I have to explain it?' [But] I realized you've got to stand up for some things."

Reflecting on the significance of a challenge being made almost 30 years after *The Chocolate War*'s publication, he added, "I feel like I must have done something right. There wouldn't be all these concerns about an ineffective book."[17]

While continuing to fight against censorship, Cormier welcomed the release of *The Bumblebee Flies Anyway* as a film in Fitchburg on March 29, 2000.[18]

Despite his productivity, Cormier's health declined after the fall that broke his back. On October 6, 2000, he entered the hospital with what appeared to be circulation problems. He was discovered to have lung cancer.

Although he returned home for a short time and continued to work on manuscripts until his death, his health rapidly deteriorated. He died in the hospital, surrounded by family, on the morning of November 2, 2000.

Cormier was remembered as a gentle, humorous and loving man who worked at honesty, maintained integrity, and was a loyal friend. His colleagues predicted that they were mourning a writer whose name would remain a mainstay in the literary world.

As an example of his loyalty and friendship, his family recalled that, throughout his career, he worked with one agent: Marilyn Marlow at Curtis Brown Ltd. in New York. She also became a good friend. He donated his papers to the local library

---

The World Remembers a Great Author

Upon hearing of his death, young adult novelist Judy Blume said, "Like the best of writers, he wrote from deep inside. He knew instinctively that if you tell a story well, respecting your characters, there is no topic that is off limits."

Fantasy writer and fellow Leominster resident, Robert A. Salvatore, recalled Cormier's encouragement: "When I got my first rejection letter in 1984 for a novel, I was devastated. I called up Bob Cormier. I didn't even know him, but he was the hometown hero. As he was answering the phone, I was thinking, 'I shouldn't even be calling this guy.'" But Cormier stayed on the phone with Salvatore for two hours offering encouragement. "He taught me how to behave when you are that successful." [19]

---

and he donated his time and service to the parish of St. Cecilia's where he was once baptized and from which he was buried.[20]

Cormier's final novel, *The Rag and Bone Shop*, was published after his death in 2001. This novel, also set in Monument, is the story of an investigator who coerces a confession of murder out of Jason Dorrant, a young boy who was the last person to see his seven-year-old neighbor, Alicia Barlett, alive. Moments after obtaining the confession, the truth is revealed: Jason is innocent and Alicia's brother murdered her.

Each year since his death, *The Chocolate War* continues to stand out amongst all the others in terms of challenges, finding its way to the third

In His Honor

In his memory, the Leominster Library opened the Robert Cormier Center for Young Adults. The area's teens, some who might recall seeing Bob Cormier visit with local retailers along the main streets, refer to it as "The Bob."

Under the leadership of the Cormier Collection's guardian, Dr. Marilyn McCafrrey, and Director Robert Foley, the Fitchburg State College library celebrates this noted author with an annual afternoon of his readings by noted faculty, researchers, and friends. His works have been read here by his family, in Japanese, and even in Croatian.[21]

spot of the American Library Association's most frequently banned books list of 2004 for sexual content, offensive language, religious viewpoint, and being unsuited to age group and violence. Cormier is listed as the second most challenged author of that year for his novels, *The Chocolate War* and *We All Fall Down*. He bears the distinction of being the second most challenged author of the decade 1990–2000.[22] Yet again, either despite the controversial nature of his books or because of it, Cormier's novel *Tenderness* has also been considered by screenwriters for a possible film. His books have already been declared young adult classics by librarians and researchers and are being read in classrooms and homes around the world each day.

In His Own Words

The following are quotes from Robert Cormier from a variety of print and Web sources, as well as personal interviews conducted by the author with the Cormier family.

On Writing

I write for the intelligent reader and this intelligent reader is often 12 or 14 or 16 years old. A work of fiction, if it is true to itself, written honestly, will set off shocks of recognition in the sensitive reader. And I write to that reader.[1]

I most enjoy novels reflecting contemporary life, characters developing in situations that demand the most from them, themes that linger long after you finish the books. Simply put, I try to write the kind of books that I like to read.[2]

I have always felt that you can have the greatest writing in the world and a terrific plot, but if your characters don't come alive, and if your reader doesn't either love them or hate them or just identify with them in some way, then everything else won't work. And so to get that sense of realism, I try to create real characters, and I think that's the key to my writing.[3]

Because young people today are exposed to so much information, they are probably more demanding in terms of realism. Yet, I think there is also an innate innocence underneath it all—kids are still kids. Styles change, slang changes, the music they love changes—but the emotions of childhood and adolescence never change.[4]

A writer can make the characters do whatever he wants. The author is the good guy and the bad guy. He must get into his character's heads. Since writers are entertainers, their characters can do what the author would never do.[5]

I love to rewrite. I love to tinker with words. I hate to let novels go when they're done. One of my novels, *Take Me Where the Good Times Are*, I actually wrote over completely after it was all done and ready to go the publisher. I sat down and did it all over again. My wife once again accused me of not wanting to let it go. I get pretty involved with the characters.[6]

Writing is like God, you create characters.[7]

On Reading

Books are probably the best of all, books that create new worlds within yourself and transport you to far places as you sit in your own den, sipping something cool in a sultry season.[8]

One of the first writers I really admired was Thomas Wolfe. I discovered him when I was in the ninth grade. . . . His prose thundered like mountain torrents. One of his dominant themes was the hunger of youth for love, fame and fortune. His themes echoed within me.[9]

I love mysteries and read them the way you'd eat popcorn.[10]

This is what writing is all about—the sweaty work of creation, the frustrating and sometimes painful putting down of words on paper to move and excite the reader.[11]

Chronology

1925—Robert Edmund Cormier born in Fitchburg, Massachusetts, on January 17.

1943—Enrolls in Fitchburg State College, Fitchburg, Massachusetts.

1944—First published short story, "The Little Things That Count" in *The Sign*.

1946—Begins work for radio station WTAG, Worcester, Massachusetts.

1948—Transfers to night staff of Leominster bureau of the *Worcester Telegram and Gazette*.

November 6: Bob Cormier and Constance Senay are married at St. Cecilia's Church in Leominister, Massachusetts, on November 6.

1951—*November 19:* Daughter Bobbie born.

1953—*August 13:* Son Peter born.

1955—Cormier moves up to the *Fitchburg Sentinel and Enterprise*.

1957—*April 6:* Daughter Chris born.

1963—*A Little Raw on Monday Mornings*.

1966—Becomes associate editor and columnist, *Fitchburg Sentinel*.

1967—*May 15:* Daughter Renee born.

1973—Best human-interest story of the year, Associated Press in New England.

1974—Column wins the K.R. Thompson award.

1977—Receives Honorary doctor of letters, Fitchburg State College.

1983—*I Am the Cheese* is made into a movie.

1988—*October 28: The Chocolate War* is made into a film and released in Los Angeles and New York as a benefit for Amnesty International.

2000—*The Bumblebee Flies Anyway* is made into a television movie.

November 2: Robert Cormier passes away.

2004—*The Chocolate War* is the third most frequently banned book of 2004 according to the American Library Association's most frequently banned books list, and Cormier is one of the ten most frequently banned authors of the decade 1990–2000.

Chapter Notes

Chapter 1. Dare to Disturb the Universe

1. Michael Cart, *From Romance to Realism: 50 Years of Growing and Change in Young Adult Literature* (New York: HarperCollins, 1996), p. 8.

2. Robert Cormier, "In His Own Words," *The Chocolate War*, 30th Anniversary Edition (New York: Alfred A. Knopf, 2002), p. 7.

3. Constance Cormier, e-mail to Ann Angel, April 24, 2005.

4. Cart, p. 8.

5. Robert Cormier, *Reflections: A Profile of Robert Cormier* (Pantheon Books, Department of Library Services, 1974), p. 2.

6. Tim Podell, *Good Conversation! A Talk with Robert Cormier*, Videotape, Tim Podell Productions, 1996.

7. Ibid.

8. Cormier, *The Chocolate War*, p. 112.

9. Podell.

10. Marie Silvaggi, "Author Tells Students: 'Just Write,'" *Daily Times Chronicle*, December 8, 1986, Cormier Collection, Fitchburg State College, Fitchburg, MA, 2006.

11. Cormier, *The Chocolate War*, pp. 142–147.

12. Robert Cormier, *Now and At The Hour* (New York: Laurel Leaf Reprint Edition, 1991), jacket copy.

13. George Snell, "Writer's Work Travels Far," *Sunday Telegram* (Leominster, Mass.), March 1997, p. B7.

14. Robert Cormier, *A Little Raw on Monday Mornings* (Laurel Leaf Reprint Edition, 1991), jacket copy.

15. Robert Cormier, *Take Me Where the Good Times Are* (Laurel Leaf Reprint Edition, 1991), jacket copy.

16. D. C. Wands, "Robert Cormier Bibliography," 2006, <http://www.fantasticfiction.co.uk/c/Robert-cormier/> (May 21, 2006).

17. Cormier, *Reflections: A Profile of Robert Cormier*, p. 2.

18. Chris Cormier Hayes, e-mail to Ann Angel, April 27, 2005.

19. Cormier, *The Chocolate War*, p. 123.

20. Podell.

21. Robert Cormier, "In His Own Words," *The Chocolate War*, p 7.

22. Cart, p. 70.

23. Constance Cormier, e-mail to Ann Angel, April 24, 2005.

24. Patricia Campbell, *Robert Cormier: Dare to Disturb the Universe* (New York: Delacorte Press, 2006), pp. 70–74.

25. Podell.

26. Robert Cormier, *Robert Cormier* (Alfred A. Knopf, Library Marketing, 1981), p. 3.

27. Renee Cormier Wheeler, e-mail to author, April 25, 2005.

28. Ibid.

29. Cart, p. 84.

30. Cormier, *Reflections: A Profile of Robert Cormier*, p. 4.

31. Ibid.

32. Ibid.

33. Constance Cormier, e-mail to Ann Angel, April 24, 2005.

34. Ibid.

35. Cormier, *Reflections: A Profile of Robert Cormier*, p. 2.

Chapter 2. Life at the Comb Factory

1. *Hayward's New England Gazetteer,* "Leominister, Massachusetts," *NewEnglandTowns.org*, 2004–2006, <http://www.newengliandtowns. org/massachusetts.leominster.html> (May 21, 2006).

2. Robert Cormier, *Portrait of a Parish, St. Cecilia's* (Leominster, Mass.: St. Cecilia's, 2000), pp. 9–18.

3. Constance Cormier, ed., "God, How I Loved that Suit," *I Have Words to Spend* (New York: Delacorte Press, 1991), p. 15.

4. Constance Cormier, ed., "Sweet Sadness," *I Have Words to Spend* (New York: Delacorte Press, 1991), p. 24.

5. Constance Cormier, e-mail interview with Ann Angel, November 2005.

6. Robert Cormier, *Fade* (New York: Delacorte Press, 1988), p. 64.

7. Constance Cormier, ed., "Sweet Sadness," p. 24.

8. D. C. Wands, "Robert Cormier Bibliography," 2006, <http://www.fantasticfiction.co.uk/c/ Robert-cormier/> (May 21, 2006).

9. Tim Podell, *Good Conversation! A Talk with Robert Cormier*, Videotape, Tim Podell Productions, 1996.

10. Chris Cormier Hayes, e-mail to Ann Angel, September 16, 2005.

11. Constance Cormier, ed., "The Heat Wave," *I Have Words to Spend*, p. 5.

12. Douglas, Jonathan. "Robert Cormier meets Melvin Burgess." *Achuka*, n.d., <http://www.achuka.co.uk/special/cormburg.htm> (January 26, 2006).

13. Robert Cormier, "Saying Thank You," *I Have Words to Spend*, p. 93.

14. Patricia J. Campbell, *Presenting Robert Cormier* (New York: Laurel-Leaf Books, 1986), pp. 17–20.

15. Robert Cormier, "The Ghost at Dusk," *I Have Words to Spend*, p. 7.

16. Robert Cormier, "A Time for Trees," *I Have Words to Spend*, p. 18.

17. Robert Cormier, "Christmas—Now and Then," *I Have Words to Spend*, p. 17.

18. Robert Cormier, "A Boy Named Pete," *I Have Words to Spend*, p. 21.

19. Constance Cormier, e-mail interview with Ann Angel, November 2005.

20. Ibid.

21. "Author Profile: Robert Cormier," *TeenReads.com*, n.d., <http://www.teenreads.com/authors/au-cormier-robert.asp> (September 7, 2006).

22. Constance Cormier, e-mail interview with Ann Angel, November 2005.

23. Ibid.

24. "Author Profile: Robert Cormier"

25. Robert Cormier, "A Boy Named Pete," pp. 20–21.

26. Constance Cormier, e-mail interview with Ann Angel, November 2005.

27. Wands, p. 1.

Chapter 3. Small Town Reporter

1. Patricia J. Campbell, *Presenting Robert Cormier* (New York: Laurel-Leaf Books, 1986), p. 20.
2. Ibid., p. 21.
3. Constance Cormier, e-mail interview with Ann Angel, November 2005.
4. Constance Cormier, personal interview at the Cormier home with Ann Angel, January 20, 2006.
5. Constance Cormier, ed., "Preface," *I Have Words to Spend* (New York: Delacorte Press, 1991), p. xiii.
6. Constance Cormier, email interview with Ann Angel, November 2005.
7. Internet Public Library, "Robert Cormier," *Kidspace@The Internet Public Library*, 1996, <http://www.ipl.org/div/kidspace/askauthor/Cormier.html> (May 21, 2006).
8. Ibid.
9. Renee Cormier Wheeler, e-mail to Ann Angel, April 24, 2005.
10. Constance Cormier, ed., "Preface," *I Have Words to Spend*, p. xiii.
11. Renee Cormier Wheeler, e-mail to Ann Angel, April 24, 2005.
12. Campbell, pp. 172–174.
13. Renee Cormier Wheeler, personal interview at the Cormier home with Ann Angel, January 20, 2006.
14. Tim Podell, *Good Conversation! A Talk with Robert Cormier*, Videotape, Tim Podell Productions, 1996.
15. Robert Cormier, "I Have Words to Spend," *I Have Words to Spend*, p. 1.

16. Dr. Wally Hastings, "Literature for Young Readers," *Northern State University*, n.d., <http://www.northern.edu/hastingw/cormier.html> (May 21, 2006).

17. Internet Public Library.

18. Constance Cormier, ed., "The Next Best Seller," *I Have Words to Spend*, p. 175.

19. Constance Cormier, ed., "Does the Melody Really Linger On?" *I Have Words to Spend*, p. 194.

20. Robert Cormier, "Should He See the Exorcist?" *I Have Words to Spend*, pp. 167–169.

21. Marilyn Marlow, "Robert Cormier Remembered," *Publishers Weekly*, January 1, 2001, p. 17.

22. Campbell, pp. 120–122.

23. Hastings, "Literature for Young Readers."

Chapter 4. The Chocolate War and Beyond

1. "Author Transforms 'Youth' Genre," *Worcester Telegram and Gazette*, p. B1, Cormier Collection, Fitchburg State College, Fitchburg, MA, 2006.

2. Constance Cormier, interview at the family home with Ann Angel, January 20, 2006.

3. Chris Cormier Wheeler, interview at the family home with Ann Angel, January 20, 2006.

4. "Author Transforms 'Youth' Genre," p. B7.

5. Pamela Mendels, "Teenage Students Find Author Speaks Their Language," *Providence Journal*, May 11, 1974, Cormier Collection.

6. Ibid.

7. Renee Cormier Wheeler, e-mail to Ann Angel, April 24, 2005.

8. Mendels.

9. Ibid.

10. Richard Nangle, "Cormier Says Writers Are Human Beings Too," *Fitchburg-Leominster Sentinel and Enterprise*, May 28, 1985, Cormier Collection.

11. Bouknight, Paula. "Author Tells Students to Start Writing," *The Middlesex News*, November 8, 1985, p. 2, Cormier Collection.

12. Ibid.

13. Maria Silvaagi, "Author Tells Students: 'Just Write,'" *Daily Times Chronicle*, December 8, 1986, Cormier Collection.

14. Jim Paulin, "Cormier Talks of Adolescent Emotions," *The Gardner News*, February 14, 1987, Cormier Collection.

15. Ibid.

16. Patricia Campbell, *Robert Cormier: Dare to Disturb the Universe* (New York: Delacorte Press, 2006), p. 4.

Chapter 5. I Am the Cheese

1. Paul Heins, "*I Am the Cheese,*" *Horn Book Magazine*. Vol. 5, August 1997, pp. 427–428, Cormier Collection, Fitchburg State College, Fitchburg, MA, 2006.

2. Phyllis Bixler, "*I Am the Cheese* and Reader-Response Criticism in the Adolescent Literature Classroom," *Webs and Wardrobes*, University Press of America, p. 13, Cormier Collection.

3. Ibid, p. 16.

4. Ibid, p. 428.

5. Colletta, Maria. "Leominster Author Pens Stunner," *Worcester Sunday Telegram*, June 19, 1977, Cormier Collection.

6. Robert R. Lingeman, "Boy in A Trap," *New York Times Book Review*, May 22, 1977, pp. 2, 51, Cormier Collection.

7. Maryanne Reynolds, "Cormier Amuses and Educates Fans at City Library Talk," *Fitchburg-Leominster Sentinel and Enterprise*, December 6, 1985, Cormier Collection.

8. Lingeman.

9. Paul Janeczko, "An Interview with Robert Cormier," *The English Journal*, September 1977, Cormier Collection.

10. Reynolds.

11. Jennifer Lord, "Area Writer Recalls Vital Role of Teachers," *Gardner News*, September 22, 1990, Cormier Collection.

12. Tim Podell, *Good Conversation! A Talk with Robert Cormier*, Videotape, Tim Podell Productions, 1996.

13. Dr. Marilyn McCaffery, et. al., *"I Am the Cheese,"* prepared by students in a graduate course taught by McCaffery, Cormier Collection.

14. Robert Foley, Cormier Collection, Fitchburg State College, Fitchburg, MA, 2006.

15. Anthony Horowitz, "Guinea-pigs," *Times Literary Supplement,* November 25, 1983, Cormier Collection.

16. Patricia Campbell, "A Loving Farewell to Robert Cormier," *Horn Book Magazine*, vol. 77, number 2, p. 246.

17. Dr. Wally Hastings, "Literature for Young Readers," *Northern State University*, n.d., <http://www.northern.edu/hastingw/cormier.html> (May 21, 2006).

18. Ibid.

Chapter 6. Censorship and Challenges

1. Gail Ciampa, "For the Author, It Feels Like a Personal Insult," *Worcester Telegram*, July 1982, Cormier Collection, Fitchburg State College, Fitchburg, MA, 2006.

2. Compton, Betty Lynn, "'Chocolate War' Author Says Ban Spurs Wrong Interest," *ACLU-SC*, May 1984, Cormier Collection.

3. Ibid.

4. Ciampa.

5. Robert Cormier, letter and essay written to Stephen Christiansen, The Children's Book Council, n.d., Cormier Collection.

6. Ibid.

7. *Voice of Youth Advocates*, vol. 8. June 1985, pp. 127–128.

8. Robert Cormier, "A Book is Not a House: The Human Side of Censorship," *Author's Insights* (Portsmouth, New Hampshire: Boynton/Cook Publishers, Inc, 1992), pp. 65–74.

9. Ibid, p. 73.

10. Ibid, 74.

11. Robert Cormier, essay for Stephen Christianson, Cormier Collection.

12. Ciampa.

13. Cormier, essay for Stephen Christianson.

14. Tim Podell, *Good Conversation! A Talk with Robert Cormier*, Videotape, Tim Podell Productions, 1996.

15. Maryanne Reynolds, "Cormier Amuses and Educates Fans at City Library Talk," *Fitchburg-Leominster Sentinel and Enterprise*, December 6, 1985, Cormier Collection.

16. Ibid.

17. Robert Cormier, Talk at the Children's Literature Association Conference, University of Missouri-Kansas City, May 16–18, 1986, Cormier Collection.

18. Ibid.

19. Ibid.

20. Michael Rosen and Pat Triggs, "Beyond the Chocolate War," *Kaleidoscope* transcript (London: British Broadcasting Corporation, November 27, 1985), Cormier Collection.

21. Ciampa.

22. Patricia J. Campbell, *Presenting Robert Cormier* (New York: Laurel-Leaf Books, 1986), pp. 160–62.

23. David Loftus, et al., "Robert Cormier Books Reviews," *AllReaders.com*, n.d., <http://www.allreaders.com/Topics/Topic_1957.asp> (January 31, 2006).

24. Patricia Campbell, "Conversing with Robert Cormier," *Amazon.com*, n.d., <http://www.amazon.com/exec/obidos/ts/feature/5191/103-8632997-7517007> (January 31, 2006).

Chapter 7. Secrets of Everyday Heroes

1. David Loftus, et al. "Robert Cormier Books Reviews," *Allreaders.com*, n.d., <http://www.allreaders.com/Topics/Topic_1957.asp> (January 31, 2006).

2. Ibid.

3. Renee Cormier Wheeler, interview at Cormier home with Ann Angel, January 20, 2006.

4. Ibid.

5. Ibid.

6. Robert Cormier, *Tunes for Bears to Dance To* (New York: Laurel Leaf, 1994).

7. Patricia Campbell, "Conversing with Robert Cormier." *Amazon.com*, n.d., <http://www.amazon.com/exec/obidos/ts/feature/5191/103-8632997-7517007> (January 31, 2006).

8. Patricia Campbell, "Conversing with Robert Cormier."

9. Cormier family, interview with Ann Angel, January 20, 2006.

10. Robert Cormier, *From the Inside Out—The Author Speaks* (New York: Alfred A. Knopf Library Marketing, 1981), p. 4.

11. Patricia Campbell, "Conversing with Robert Cormier."

12. Loftus.

Chapter 8. Cormier's Readers Change Over Time

1. Paul Jancezko, "An Interview with Robert Cormier," *The English Journal*, September 1977, p. 11, Cormier Collection, Fitchburg State College, Fitchburg, MA, 2006.

2. Cormier family interview with Ann Angel, January 20, 2006.

3. Paul Jancezko, "An Interview with Robert Cormier."

4. Ibid.

5. Patricia Campbell, *Reader's Companion: Tenderness* (New York: Delacorte Press, n.d.), p. 4.

6. Ibid.

7. Patricia Campbell, "Conversing with Robert Cormier," *Amazon.com*, n.d., <http://www.amazon.com/exec/obidos/ts/feature/5191/103-8632997-7517007> (January 31, 2006).

8. David Loftus, et al. "Robert Cormier Books Reviews," *Allreaders.com*, n.d., <http://www.allreaders.com/Topics/Topic_1957.asp> (January 31, 2006).

9. Patricia Campbell, "Conversing with Robert Cormier."

10. Ibid.

11. Family Interview with Ann Angel, January 20, 2006.

12. Loftus.

13. Lyn Gardner, "Robert Cormier," *Guardian Unlimited*, November 6, 2000, <http://books.guardian.co.uk/news/articles/0,6109,393333,00.html> (January, 13, 2006).

14. Lisa Gerson, "Try a Little Tenderness," City Journal, *Boston Magazine*, December 1997, pp. 9–10.

15. Ibid., p. 151.

16. Gardner.

17. The Associated Press, "*Chocolate War* Author Battles Effort to Ban Book," *freedomforum.org*, n.d., <http://www.freedomforum.org/templates/document.asp?documented=12693& printerfriendsly=1> (January 14, 2006).

18. Patricia Campbell, *Daring to Disturb the Universe* (New York: Delacorte Press, 2006), p. 283.

19. Margaret Smith, "Fellow Authors Reminisce about Cormier," *Sentinel and Enterprise*, November 5, 2000, Cormier Collection.

20. Cormier family interview with Ann Angel, January 20, 2006.

21. Ibid.

22. American Library Association. "Challenged and Banned Books," *ALA website on Intellectual Freedom*, n.d., <www.ala.org/ala/oif/ bannedbooksweek/challengedbanned/ channengedbanned.htm> (May 28, 2005).

In His Own Words

1. Renee Cormier Wheeler, e-mail to Ann Angel, April 24, 2005.

2. Robert Cormier, *From the Inside Out—The Author Speaks* (New York: Alfred A. Knopf Library Marketing, 1981), p. 2.

3. Patricia Campbell, *Reader's Companion: Tenderness* (New York: Delacorte Press, n.d.), p. 6.

4. "Author Profile: Robert Cormier," *TeenReads.com*, n.d., <http://www.teenreads.com/authors/ au-cormier-robert.asp> (September 7, 2006).

5. Maria Silvaagi, "Author Tells Students: 'Just Write,'" *Daily Times Chronicle,* December 8, 1986, Cormier Collection, Fitchburg State College, Fitchburg, MA, 2006.

6. Paul Janeczko, "An Interview with Robert Cormier," *The English Journal*, September 1977, Cormier Collection.

7. Jim Paulin, "Cormier Talks of Adolescent Emotions," *The Gardner News*, February 14, 1987, Cormier Collection.

8. Constance Cormier, ed., "The Next Best Seller," *I Have Words to Spend* (New York: Delacorte Press, 1991), p. 175.

9. Robert Cormier, *From the Inside Out—The Author Speaks.*, p. 4.

10. Ibid.

11. Robert Cormier, "A Book is Not a House: The Human Side of Censorship," *Author's Insights* (Portsmouth, New Hampshire: Boynton/Cook Publishers, Inc., 1992), p. 68.

Glossary

advent—To come into being; to begin.

autobiographical—The biography of a person as written by him or herself.

censorship—The practice of keeping certain information from being circulated.

challenged book—A book that a person or group demands be taken out of circulation in a classroom, library, or bookstore.

deterministic—The theory that an act of will is caused by preceding events.

fictionalize—To create a story from the imagination.

incongruity—An idea or scene that lacks conformity or harmony.

indifference—An absence of care or concern.

Industrial Revolution—Changes in the economy during the late eighteenth century that were brought about by the development of power-driven machinery.

omniscient—A narrator with complete or universal knowledge.

prolific—Abundant inventiveness or productivity.

psychological thriller—Emotionally charged novel that offers suspense, adventure, and intrigue.

self-deprecating—To make little of a talent or
   ability.

semi-autobiographical—Partly autobiographical.

stillborn—The state of having died prior to, or
   moments after birth; a failure to begin.

triple-deckers—Apartment buildings, also called
   tenements, that contained three separate
   dwellings or apartments, stacked one on top of
   the other.

voracious—Delight in eating or acquiring things
   such as acquiring the information and
   knowledge found in books.

Selected Works

Novels:

Now and At the Hour (1960)
A Little Raw on Monday Mornings (1963)
Take Me Where the Good Times Are (1965)
The Chocolate War (1974)
I Am the Cheese (1977)
After the First Death (1979)
The Bumblebee Flies Away (1983)
Beyond the Chocolate War (1985)
Fade (1988)
Other Bells for Us to Ring (1990)
We All Fall Down (1991)
Tunes for Bears to Dance To (1992)
In the Middle of the Night (1995)
Tenderness (1997)
Heroes (1998)
Frenchtown Summer (1999)
The Rag and Bone Shop (2001)

Collections:

Eight Plus One (1980)

Nonfiction:

I Have Words to Spend (1991)

Further Reading

Hipple, Ted, ed. *Writers for Young Adults*. New York: Scribner, 1997.

Hyde, Margaret O. *Robert Cormier*. Broomall, Pa.: Chelsea House, 1999.

Keeley, Jennifer. *Understanding* I Am the Cheese. San Diego, Cal.: Lucent Books, 2001.

Thomson, Sarah L. *Robert Cormier.* New York: Rosen Publishing Group, 2003.

Wilson, Kathleen, ed. *Major 20th-Century Writers: A Selection of Sketches from Contemporary Authors*. Farmington Hills, Mich.: Gale Group, 1998.

Internet Addresses

Author Profile: Robert Cormier
http://www.teenreads.com/authors/
au-cormier-robert.asp

Kidsreads.com—Robert Cormier
http://www.kidsreads.com/authors/
au-cormier-robert.asp

ML Author Spotlight—Robert Cormier
http://www.classzone.com/novelguides/
authors/cormier.cfm

Index